LOATHE THY NEIGHBOUR

LOATHE THY NEIGHBOUR

JAMES O'BRIEN

LEADING BRITAIN'S CONVERSATION
DAB DIGITAL RADIO | 97.3 FM

First published 2015 by
Elliott and Thompson Limited
27 John Street
London WC1N 2BX
www.eandtbooks.com

ISBN: 978-1-78396-086-6

Text © James O'Brien 2015

The views expressed in this book are the views of the author
and do not necessarily reflect the views of Global Radio.

All rights reserved. No part of this publication may be
reproduced, stored in or introduced into a retrieval system,
or transmitted, in any form, or by any means (electronic,
mechanical, photocopying, recording or otherwise) without
the prior written permission of the publisher. Any person who
does any unauthorised act in relation to this publication may be
liable to criminal prosecution and civil claims for damages.

9 8 7 6 5 4 3 2 1

A catalogue record for this book is available from the
British Library.

Managing Editor, LBC: James Rea
Deputy Managing Editor, LBC: Tom Cheal

Typesetting: Marie Doherty
Printed in the UK by TJ International Ltd

'Owe no one anything, except to love one another; for the one who loves another has fulfilled the law. The commandments, "You shall not commit adultery; You shall not murder; You shall not steal; You shall not covet;" and any other commandment, are summed up in this word, "Love your neighbour as yourself." Love does no wrong to a neighbour; therefore, love is the fulfilling of the law.'

THE LETTER OF SAINT PAUL TO THE ROMANS

'Be excellent to each other.'

TED 'THEODORE' LOGAN AND BILL S. PRESTON, ESQUIRE, *BILL AND TED'S EXCELLENT ADVENTURE*

Contents

Introduction   xi

1 The boy who cried wolf   1
2 When is an immigrant not an immigrant? 13
3 The immigrant next door   23
4 The last refuge of a scoundrel   35
5 'You can't talk about immigration …'   47
6 If the cap fits   57
7 Infidel-ity   67
8 Taking the biscuit   79

Introduction

This may not be among the best ideas I've ever come up with. To suggest, even tentatively, that constant conversations about 'immigration' and the problems it purportedly provides might be a much, much more profound social problem than the issue itself will, in the current climate, seem to many to be an act of reckless provocation.

The same result, with a lot less effort, could no doubt be achieved by painting a target on my backside and inviting all comers to take pot shots at my posterior until I take back the ludicrous assertion that our country would be a happier, healthier, more harmonious place if we stopped the immigration conversation altogether.

Neither will my cause be helped much by offering a long-forgotten 1990s craze for optical illusions as our starting point but it is, at least, better than no starting point at all. Just.

The 'Magic Eye' illustrations, by which the

nation was briefly but comprehensively seduced in about 1991, left an indelible impression on me. The idea was simple: stare at an apparently random series of squiggles and scrawls for long enough, unfocus your eyes from what was on the page and instead concentrate on what was 'behind' it, and a full, detailed drawing of anything from an ocean liner to a lion's head would somehow swim into your vision. Blink and it would be gone again.

I never once achieved satisfaction. Despite looking at hundreds of them, hoping that this time the meaningless scribbles would coalesce into something recognisable, there never came the vaguest hint of the artist's hidden intention. If it wasn't for the fact that just about everybody else on the planet managed to get the hang of it, it would have been tempting to chalk the whole thing up as a lucrative con.

There is something about immigration debates at the moment that puts me in mind of those Magic Eyes. It is a sense that if we stare for long enough at the thoughts of people whose positions are angry, critical and fearful then we might unlock what it is they see and somehow help them to a happier, more peaceful place.

And vice versa, if it is actually true that deep reservations about and objections to immigration can be fostered in breasts untainted by racism or xenophobia, then staring at the squiggles — or listening to the radio broadcasts — of someone like me might help assuage all that unnecessary fear, soothe that unquenchable anger.

It may seem a strange analogy, never mind a strange ambition, but two things are certain in this arena: facts offer no meaningful opposition to feelings, and conversations involving opposing attitudes to the ebb and flow of people across our borders rarely, if ever, leave interlocutors feeling better, happier, more at one with the world than they did at the discussion's beginning. Ordinarily, we all feel considerably worse.

If you are married to the notion that your country is heading hellwards in a handcart because of the presence in it of too many people from foreign climes, you will be enraged and often offended at even the suggestion that you're wrong. Conversely, if you believe that most of the arguments against immigration are bogus and most of the more prominent arguers are, at best, self-serving charlatans and, at worst, fomenters of racial hatred, then you will be left depressed at the ease with which so many people who deserve neither of these criticisms have been persuaded into the same school of thought.

What, plausibly, do you think would happen if we never talked about immigration again? If we treated a person's geographical origins with the same insouciance we currently apply to their star sign? If, in other words, we no more considered immigrants to be responsible for our society's perceived flaws than we do families with more than two children or people who choose to work harder than their colleagues?

It's not easy. You're staring at my squiggles now but there's probably no hint of a cogent image behind them. Sadly, I don't have a Rosetta stone to unlock what seems obvious to some but downright treacherous to others: that the real enemies of a country's happiness and health are not the people who come to it in search of improved existences, but the people who insist that they shouldn't.

But imagine if the demagogues and scaremongers of immigration were to transfer their ire to other targets and just see how absurd their assertions would appear. It has, for example, become popular in Europe recently for far-right politicians to conjure up images of unbearable national futures by detailing in suitably apocalyptic terms what is statistically possible but (they never add) wholly and laughably implausible.

There is, one of them might say, nothing to prevent 400 gazillion people currently resident in other EU member states from moving to France/Germany/Britain etc. tomorrow. This is demonstrably true. No matter that there is nothing to stop every resident of France/Germany/Britain moving elsewhere either; the siege mentality is served by describing barbarians at the gate, not by pointing out that open gates admit two-way traffic. You might take issue with the use of 'gazillion' here, but it represents the total number of people currently alive in the relevant area and so theoretically entitled to up sticks tomorrow.

They put leaflets through your letterbox in which 'Unless we change our laws 400 gazillion Romanians/Bulgarians/Frenchmen could move to your town/country/street tomorrow!' is picked out in bolder, bigger type than anything else on the page and they sow a seed of suspicion in a heartbreakingly high number of minds that this deluge could conceivably occur. It won't, of course, but by the time tomorrow comes it doesn't matter. The politician, the columnist, the pundit has already established herself as someone who understands, nay, champions the fears of people worried about the imminent possible arrival of 400 gazillion foreign folk. Intellectually, you might as well be promising to slay dragons. Emotionally, you're in clover, a veritable champion of the fearful and misled.

Here, then, are some other equally true assertions about the relationship between population, peace and prosperity: 'Unless we forcibly sterilise every woman in this country of child-bearing age, the total population could be 400 gazillion by the Christmas after next!' Or: 'There is literally nothing to stop every man, woman and child in your country moving to Norwich/Nantes/Nuremberg tomorrow!' and finally: 'Unless we change our laws, every adult in the country could spend the rest of their lives drunk. There would be nobody sober to teach your children or treat your illnesses.'

Pick a favourite, they all serve the same purpose: to highlight how absurd it would be in almost any other imaginable scenario to allow something that could theoretically happen to be escalated into a warning that it certainly will. Who benefits from this escalation? Well, find me a politician, columnist or pundit that isn't either paid handsomely for fostering these fears or articulating their own ugly prejudices or, more usually, both, and I will eat my sandals.

They benefit handsomely. We don't. We end up frightened and angry if we buy their snake oil; depressed and despairing if we don't. Compared to the people who are actually the targets of this fraudulent and divisive rhetoric, though, compared to immigrants or people who 'look like' immigrants or people who 'might be' immigrants, we are both getting off lightly.

The job of these tub-thumping charlatans is made even easier if there's a natural upturn in the waxing and waning of population. Recession or similar conspires to create a hatemonger's hat-trick: charismatic demagogue; domestic economic difficulty; and increased arrivals from abroad.

For while it may defy all logic to suggest that people with less than us are responsible for the shortfalls and flaws in our own lives, history teaches that we will take up an invitation to blame them for our unhappiness with a lot more alacrity than one to blame people above us in the food chain.

That is the history of pogroms, of lynchings,

of signs in boarding-house windows stating: 'No Dogs, No Blacks, No Irish'. And it is a history that repeats itself with chilling inevitability generation after generation after generation, because the immigration conversation may change in pitch and tone and context but it never changes in content. It is always about people urging us to judge each other by what we are not, not what we do, by where we're from, not where we're going, and by the contents of our birth certificates, not the contents of our hearts and minds. And it is a conversation always started by people poised to grow fat on a diet of hatred and division that starves the rest of us of compassion, of logic, of simple humanity.

These are some of my squiggles. More follow, random in places but entirely sincere. I would be grateful if you could take the time to stare at them for a while longer but apologise in advance if nothing meaningful or helpful or new emerges while you do!

1
The boy who cried wolf

LOATHE THY NEIGHBOUR

Do you remember the boy who cried wolf? Of course you do. His story has been told through the ages to caution us against the dangers of raising false alarms. Do so too often, we learn, and you will not be believed when finally, and for the first time, your warning is urgent and real.

Take another look at the tale now, though, and ask yourself whether that message really holds true. The boy becomes bored watching over sheep that belong to his fellow villagers. Apart, presumably, from a few minor responsibilities for ovine health and safety, his sole job is to ring a bell at the first sight of a wolf and so alert those villagers to the imminent danger and bring them at breakneck speed to the field to ward off the wolf.

It is, in many ways, an important job for a youngster. At least on paper it is. He is charged with safeguarding not just livestock but livelihoods. Allow a wolf to rampage through the flock and people will go hungry, wool unsold, cutlets uncut. Neither is it work without risk. If he were ever to go nose to snout with a snarling, ravenous wolf, only a fool would bet on the boy prevailing.

Off paper, however, it all looks pretty dull. Unless the bell is actually rung, the boy might as well not exist. His days in many ways have less purpose than those of even the sheep he guards. Important he may be in theory, but in practice he is effectively impotent, irrelevant unless danger actually arrives. Were he, for example, to announce grandly every evening that yet another day had passed wolf-free, he would be more or less ignored. This status quo is not exciting; it is not particularly interesting. By definition, a status quo just is.

So he shatters it. He rings the bell; he sounds the alarm; he brings the villagers running to the field and delights in their panic and excitement. He matters. He is noticed. He is no longer bored.

So the next day he does it again, and the next day, and the one after that, until eventually the villagers get wise to his wheeze and ignore an alarm he has, for once, sounded sincerely. Their incredulity leaves the boy — and their sheep — to become wolf lunch.

There is no second chapter to the story. We are supposed to learn a simple lesson and adjust our moral compass accordingly. But should we? Why, for example, is the story focused upon the boy who cried wolf rather than the villagers who heard his cry?

Imagine now that we are the villagers. That we see our futures, our fortunes, our very survival inextricably tied up with the safety of our flock and we see the wolf — the interloper, the invader — as a permanent threat to our personal and material security. Can you really imagine a day on which the bell would ring and we ignore it, blithely running the risk of annihilation because we don't trust the adolescent shepherd any more? Of course not.

No matter that no wolf has been seen in these parts for years: threats are rarely about reality and our reactions to unreal threats are rarely rational. No matter how many times the boy's alarm proved false on previous occasions, or how often he claimed that the wolf had fled mere moments before we arrived mob-handed, surely we would never ignore the bell. The risk would be too great. The more we have invested in what is threatened, the more we fear its destruction. The fear of what the wolf represents is too deeply imbedded in our collective psyche to be ignored.

That's where the boy who cried wolf went wrong. If he wanted to continue enlivening and validating his own existence, he should have adopted different tactics. He should never have allowed the villagers to see through his ruse. Instead of sniggering at their gullibility, he should have nurtured it, fed it and watched it flower.

No matter that no actual evidence of a wolf was available. Fear deals more with feelings than with facts and the villagers' fears could have been easily stoked with tales of wolfish carnage wreaked upon a flock on a nearby hill, or with tales of the gratuitous violence inflicted upon a neighbouring village. Depending upon the era in which our story unfolds, he could paint bloody pictures of savaged sheep on a cave wall or download from the Internet old images taken on the other side of the world and claim they were in fact taken after a wolf attack in the next valley. Yesterday.

A witness would be ideal now: someone to lie through their teeth about the proximity of an especially murderous pack. Someone to praise the boy's vigilance and underline his importance while passing his cap around the cowed villagers in pursuit of payment for the risks he has run by coming here.

Then he could throw in some statistics to back up his story. The accuracy of Mark Twain's famous dictum about 'lies, damned lies and statistics' is apparently not obvious to everyone. The keener or more conditioned you are to believe what the statistics 'prove', the less likely you are to question them. Surely, you say, some statistical 'facts' are just that: inviolate and incontestable. Maybe they are. Let me know when you find some. Mostly their impact seems defined by the motives of the person citing them.

'The average rural wolf attack', the boy might argue, 'leaves seventy sheep, two humans and six fluffy kittens dead in unspeakable circumstances. They kill for fun, not just for food, you know, and it is well known that they urinate in wells and water troughs in order to poison water supplies.

'There are', he might explain, 'thirty-seven wolves currently known to be at large in the immediate vicinity of our village, but they breed like rabbits, of course, and there could well be two hundred by Christmas. Not only that, the borders of our village are unpatrolled (except by little old me) so there is literally nothing (except little old me) to stop every wolf on the continent (and beyond if they're strong swimmers — and some of them are!) taking up residence here tomorrow.'

Are there any facts in this narrative? Sort of, but it really doesn't matter. Remember what it is designed to do: shore up the boy's importance, validate his existence, alleviate his boredom and camouflage his feelings of inadequacy. All of this is achieved by frightening his fellows as much as possible. 'I matter', he is telling the villagers, 'precisely because the threat of wolves is so acute, and just because you haven't seen any doesn't mean they aren't there. Do you really want to risk the same fate as that village I told you about where everyone was eaten, or end up like those decapitated fluffy kittens I showed you pictures of?'

With a slightly different modus operandi, then, the boy who cried wolf would not have ended up dead and disbelieved, he would have ended up with a pay rise. Indeed, if he was possessed of a little charisma and a plausible demeanour, he could probably have gotten himself elected mayor of the village on an anti-wolf ticket.

Any population sufficiently persuaded of an imminent threat to their security or general wellbeing is, whether or not that threat even exists, putty in the hands of a skilled propagandist. The boy who cried wolf didn't need a lesson in honesty, he just needed better PR.

Of course, in the original tale the wolf did actually exist. The danger, though no doubt exaggerated by the boy's false alarms, was ultimately real and present.

Imagine, now, that the boy had discovered soon after starting his subterfuge that there were in fact no wolves, that wolves were extinct. Where would he be if this became common knowledge? Far from being the doughty protector of the village, a veritable wolf-whisperer with more apparent knowledge of the animal than men three times his age, he would instantly become a boy in a field full of sheep with no status at all, no purpose to serve save untangling the odd ewe from a prickly hedgerow.

Do you think he would tell us the truth? Of course he wouldn't. To do so would be to render himself ridiculous, to expose his own ludicrous exaggerations and self-serving lies. For while the wolf might not be real, the people's fear and anger indubitably are, and as long as he can feel and feed those emotions, the boy has power. And it is a power so seductive that we should not be surprised if a little cognitive dissonance comes into play and our little anti-hero actually comes to believe in the non-existent wolf. Who, after all, would really want dragons actually to exist except the self-styled dragon-slayer?

That, it seems to me, is the nature of the so-called 'immigration debate' today. People are not influenced by demonstrable facts or experiences but by fallacious anecdotes and rampaging feelings, and those feelings are fanned daily by people whose personal success — whether through selling newspapers, seeking political power or attracting listeners to a radio phone-in show — increases every time we feel scared or angry or both.

The last thing these people want us to do is wonder whether there is, really, anything to be scared of at all. And these 'plain-speakers', these tellers of 'truths', these self-styled dragon-slayers will stop at almost nothing to silence and ridicule the people who tell us that there is absolutely nothing to be scared of, to tell us that there is no wolf.

2
When is an immigrant not an immigrant?

If a man were to push you from the path of a speeding car, how much store would you set by his country of origin or even his immigration status? Seriously, can you conceive of any circumstances in which your gratitude to the man who saved your life would be in any way influenced or diluted by his nationality or ethnicity or colour? That you would feel somehow less thankful, less lucky, less indebted if he turned out to be from Poland or Pakistan or Peru as opposed to Preston, Pitlochrie or Penge?

These are, of course, intended to be rhetorical questions. Certainly, there are still people around who would recoil at the thought of even being touched by the wrong type of foreigner but they are, I fear, probably beyond the reach of the reasoned argument or, perhaps more accurately, the clumsy but well-meaning philosophy being employed here ...

It is, then, fair to say that almost all of us would find the idea of objecting to having our life saved on the grounds of our saviour's ethnicity palpably absurd. It simply does not matter.

In the context of the wider story it is precisely as important and as relevant as his star sign or the football team he supports or the colour of the socks he was wearing.

So why are insidious invitations to set enormous store by the nationality of the car's *driver* routinely taken up with a truly ugly alacrity? The offending driver's colour, creed or country of origin is surely of no more relevance to our situation than the Good Samaritan's (deliberate biblical reference there, at least part of the point of that parable is the point of this chapter). If we don't care about the foreignness of our rescuer, why on earth are we so easily persuaded to care passionately about the foreignness of our 'attacker'?

You have seen the headlines, possibly without even realising what was happening: 'Romanian driver crashes into bus stop queue'; 'Asylum seeker sought after hit and run outside school' et cetera. What place, precisely, do nationality and immigration status have in such stories? What possible purpose is served by their inclusion? Have you, for example, ever seen them similarly cited in the headlines of news reports that could be usefully described as 'happy'? 'Immigrant rescues stranded child', perhaps, or 'Bulgarian saves the day'? Maybe we could find one or two if we searched hard enough but nobody can dispute the fundamental imbalance here: foreignness only really matters when the foreigner does naughty things. When the foreigner does nice things he's not really a foreigner at all.

Consider a recent case in America where a student with no immigration documentation (a fairly reliable indicator of illegality) won a scholarship to a college. Fox News Latino, which caters for a largely Hispanic audience, reported the story under the headline 'In rare move, university grants $22K scholarship to undocumented student.' Over at Fox News, which caters for a largely non-Hispanic and historically 'right-wing' audience, the exact same story, accompanied by the exact same photograph of the exact same young student, appeared under the headline: 'Money for illegals'. The two television stations, as the name suggests, are part of the same organisation.

This case highlights perfectly the way in which, with particular reference to feeding xenophobic tendencies which may often be unconscious, much of modern media has completely and deliberately blurred the line between report and comment, between the providing of facts and the prompting of emotional response which invariably involves pandering to prejudice. And, of course, for every reader, viewer or listener whose prejudices are being pandered to there will be another for whom the same prejudices will be forming afresh in her consciousness. The 'journalism', in other words, is deliberately designed to feed that feeling of the amorphous constituency of 'foreigners' or 'immigrants' being somehow up to no good.

Would you really care about the geographical origin of the doctor who gave you the all clear, or the shopkeeper who returned your lost purse or the teacher who helped your children achieve their potential? So why would you care about the country of origin of a doctor you were unhappy with, or a shopkeeper who short-changed you or a teacher who marked your children's homework badly?

We are all guilty here. I am certainly not adopting a holier-than-thou approach to feeling prickles of prejudice when confronted with someone whose 'otherness' might provide a convenient hook upon which to hang an anger-assuaging insult. If you get cut up by an overweight person while driving there follows an often irresistible impulse to shout at the 'fat bastard'. You might, of course, hold magnificently enlightened views on the issue of obesity and believe passionately that sufferers from it need help and understanding rather than abuse and name-calling but, in the heat of that moment in traffic, the other driver's fatness is the most obvious weapon to hand which might be employed to hurt him.

And that seems to me to be of huge importance. When we are enraged or annoyed or even just noticeably irritated by another person and want to lash out, to hurt, to cause them mental anguish, we reach for words we think will work *regardless of whether we hold the views the words convey.* Substitute the word 'fat' here for 'black' or 'Polish' and I think you'll see what I'm getting at. It would, of course, be a racist act to shout 'You black bastard!' at someone who had annoyed you (just, I suppose, as it would be to shout 'You white bitch!'), but it is by no means certain, or even likely, that the shouter is in fact a racist person.

Anything that marks your temporary enemy out as 'other' offers itself as an effective means with which to hurt them. Colour and weight, as we have seen, most obviously fit the bill but the list is almost endless: height, sexuality, ugliness, hair colour, clothing ... All speak of an ugly little impulse within us all (my apologies if you feel exempt from this observation, but you're probably kidding yourself) to use someone's minority status as a weapon. Once we are aware of this appetite within us we have a choice: to feed it and so increase the anger in our lives, or to resist the siren call of 'Money for illegals' and 'Romanian driver kills pedestrian' rhetoric and so hopefully quieten the ugly voice within.

More worryingly, though, that ugly little voice is not confined to situations in which the 'immigrant' has deliberately done us harm. Hospital and doctors' waiting rooms are probably the best place to recognise the grim truth of this. If you are obliged to wait for longer than you would like — and you invariably will be — it seems almost impossible not to question the rights of other people present to be seen before you. It is here that even ostensibly liberal people might find themselves unhappily clocking thick accents, or niqabs, or the colour of complexions (no matter that this no longer provides even the vaguest indication of non-nativeness). It is almost a reflex action. But not quite, because you can catch yourself doing it, you can recognise the reality of what I describe and you can make a choice: do I indulge the enraging but irrelevant detail of my fellow patients' ethnicity or do I afford it exactly the same importance as I do the ethnicity of my doctors and nurses?

'The boy who cried wolf' has shown us that the appeal of invitations to be frightened or angry or both depends largely on how much we have invested in that which is supposedly under threat from the 'wolf'. Nothing fits this bill more perfectly than our essential personal safety, our physical wellbeing, our very health. These, by definition, are the things we feel most protective of. So a columnist or pundit or phone-in host who feeds the fear that they are somehow under threat from 'foreigners' is guaranteed our attention regardless of how reasonable that fear may be — and regardless of how much damage to community cohesion, to society itself, feeding that fear may wreak.

So while it's no more relevant than his star sign or the football team he supports, a criminal's foreignness is rendered headline news, an ineluctable fact that often seems to be afforded more weight and condemnation than the crime itself. At risk of being inappropriately brutal, do you really think a rape victim is even the tiniest bit bothered by the ethnicity of her attacker? Of course she isn't. So why does so much media coverage of crime these days suggest that *we* should be? And why on earth are we so easily persuaded that it matters? Because once the foundation stones of fear and anger have been laid, scaremongers and demagogues can build almost anything they like upon them. And they will.

It is only here where ugly prejudices are fed by 'professionals' grown fat on the fear and fury of their consumers that the nationality of the speeding car's driver somehow matters more than the nationality of the man who pushed you from its path.

3
The immigrant next door

When is an immigrant not part of the immigration problem? The short answer to that question is, quite often, when you know the immigrant personally. It's the stuff of cliché and outdated comedy routines but we do regularly fail to see that negative racial generalisations unintentionally encompass our friends. Even, believe it or not, our families.

Someone, for instance, might start telling a racist joke in the pub and not realise that there's a friend present who, to all intents and purposes, it would apply to. This is the rhetoric of 'Obviously I don't mean him. It's all the others that are causing the problems.' Or, in a previous era, 'Not you, Chalky, you're all right!'

I remember a caller to my radio show during the salad days of the fascistic British National Party who was adamant that a draconian programme of colour-based repatriation, apartheid and internment was the only way to solve our nation's ills. 'And you can't call me racist,' he insisted, 'I've got mixed-race grandchildren and I love them.'

One of the most enduringly fascinating

aspects of the British National Party and their successors in British politics (there always seems to be at least one group of race-obsessed white people falsely claiming to be concerned only by 'immigration levels' while enjoying varying degrees of profile and popularity according to the economic situation of the nation and the clubbability of their leaders) is looking at the territory where they enjoy most traction. In short, in areas where immigration is high, the original population report the least concerns and in areas where it is low to non-existent, the natives are most exercised.

In many ways, the immigration debate should end right here. Point out to people with little or no experience of the tides of immigration flowing in and out of their lives that people who actually live on the beach are supremely unconcerned by it and you should, in a logical universe, quell all their concerns and assuage all of their fears. But you won't. Partly because a certain type of politician profits from propagating the anger and fear as much as, if not more than, journalists and commentators do; and partly because we often don't think of actual people when the word 'immigrants' is barked at us in the right (by which, of course, I mean wrong) way — we think of a massive, faceless mob of problems.

It is a self-perpetuating circle of unhappiness that extremists and far-right politicians have been drawing on for generations. The more multicoloured a community, the less hung up on colour it will be. The more multifarious a population, the less susceptible it will be to the suggestion that the black/brown/Irish/Eastern Europeans living just over there want to steal your sausages. So the politicians and pundits whose very livelihoods depend upon sustaining the fear and anger we feel toward the faceless sausage-thieves very deliberately look the other way.

They talk of 'metropolitan elites' instead of 'communities where immigration is highest' as being somehow insulated from or ignorant of the concerns of 'ordinary people'. By 'ordinary', of course, they mean people who have little or no experience of the things they are hoping to use to terrify them into voting. It is a neat semantic trick that masks the contempt in which far-right politicians often hold the people on whom they depend for votes and attention. 'Ordinary' here translates as 'gullible', 'closed-minded' and 'ignorant' as opposed to 'clear-eyed', 'experienced' and 'open-minded'.

It seems an unkind analysis, but how else can we explain such things as Nigel Farage's tirades against children who speak foreign languages at home, or adults who do so in public, or foreign workers who take 'British' jobs, while his own wife and children fit every single one of these bills quite perfectly? He is either too stupid to realise his own hypocrisy or has persuaded himself that his supporters are too cowed and stupid to care about it. Neither explanation is pretty.

So we live in a country where concerns about immigration are highest among people who know the least about it, and lowest among people for whom it is as much a part of daily reality as breakfast or public transport. We're not special, incidentally. Throughout history and all across the world, it was ever thus. And if history won't be heeded, is there any point even trying to unravel such counter-intuitive absurdity? Or do we have to wait until immigrants reach the corners of the country currently untouched and deliver the message personally that they are really nothing to worry about?

In all honesty, I don't know, but it's worth exploring both exactly why familiarity breeds content among the masses and why even people possessed of fairly grim perspectives regarding race and ethnicity frequently fail to see the people they actually know as part of the perceived problem. It's also worth remembering here that this is an exercise as much in helping people who are hindered and hidebound by all the effort put into frightening them as it is the people they are being encouraged to be frightened of.

It is this faceless, amorphous, almost always

negatively portrayed constituency of 'immigrants' that speaks loudest to our innate fear of any external threat to our status quo. And yet it does not, in any truly meaningful sense, exist. There is no such thing as 'immigrants'. There are no unifying traits or behaviours, no unanimously shared objectives or beliefs, no defining characteristics. There is no 'immigrants' way to do anything and no 'immigrants' attitude to anything. There is no 'immigrants' answer to any given question and no 'immigrants' response to any given situation. There is not even an 'immigrants' attitude to immigration itself. There are just people: diverse, different and distinct. It makes no more sense to talk of them as a specific, cohesive entity responsible for specific, defined societal events than it would to speak similarly of the curly-haired or of Capricorns.

When we hear tell, then, of what 'immigrants' do, what they are responsible for, what they represent, we are already lost to logical analysis. People with relaxed attitudes to immigration understand this because they do not have much room in their minds for a concept of 'immigrants' as opposed to just 'people'. The room is already taken up with their colleagues, their children's classmates, shopkeepers, doctors, bus drivers, families, friends. We do not judge these people according to where they come from but according to what they do, and we find, unremarkably, that what they do is, for the most part, no different from anybody else.

You can't really be frightened by them or by tales of the horrors they represent, because you know them. You know that your friends and colleagues and acquaintances from sunnier or colder climes are not responsible for any of the problems laid at the door of 'immigrants'. You know that even if some clothing or customs or habits can be arresting the first few times you encounter them, you will soon cease to register them at all. Like living under a flight path and only really noticing the noise when people come to visit and point it out, living among immigrants is just living. Apart, of course, from people determined never to be persuaded from their beliefs in racial inferiority (and why are the poster boys for such master-race rhetoric so obviously and so often drawn from the very bottom of their own gene pool?), everybody gets this eventually. You have to. Living among 'immigrants', for the people who actually do it, is just living. For many of the people who don't, alas, it still represents a terrible and terrifying future.

Some people want to be frightened. They thrive on anger and division and upset. Some people want to be poorly. Psychologists have given them a name. Some people want to be none of the above and it is they who are most let down, most insulted by the immigration 'debate'. Anecdotes, hollow and often fraudulent 'statistics', exaggerations, unrepresentative examples and often outright lies all conspire to make it heartbreakingly difficult for these people to see the unnecessary upset being deliberately inflicted upon them. It's for their sake that it's worth pointing out that 'anti-immigration' politicians play best where there isn't any immigration; that there are two narratives available, one negative, one positive. The negative immigration narrative is the one told by people who don't live with it to people who don't; the positive — or, to be honest, the often utterly ambivalent narrative — is told by the people who do live with it. The latter narrative is also known as the truth.

Are you one of these people? It is a simple enough question of who or what pops into your head when you hear the word 'immigrants'. You will think either of friends, colleagues, neighbours and professionals: people with names, job descriptions, roles in your world, faces. Or you will think of a hundred and numpty thousand (depending on the latest headline/speech on the subject) faceless, nameless school place shortages or hospital waiting lists or court translation services. And the sort of language ordinarily reserved for the faceless, nameless ones is only permissible because it sidesteps the fact that we are talking about real individuals and focuses instead on an amorphous mass. 'They' do this; 'they' think that; 'they' breed like rabbits; 'they' smell.

There is no 'they'. There is only 'we'.

4
The last refuge of a scoundrel

Dr Samuel Johnson's famous description of patriotism as the last refuge of a scoundrel was, according to his biographer Boswell, first coined in 1775. Nearly 250 years later it came to mind as I strolled into Hyde Park in London with my young family for one of the many official celebrations of Queen Elizabeth's Diamond Jubilee. It was more than just a jamboree. Following fast upon the pageantry, ceremony and near hysteria that accompanied the previous year's wedding of her grandson Prince William in 2011, it marked a kind of restoration of regal authority. Cracks and fissures that had plagued the monarchy since their allegedly inadequate reaction to the death of William's mother, Diana, had been filled, and quasi-constitutional problems prompted by the 'eccentricities' of his father, Prince Charles, seemed to have been solved.

It made for a heady mix and everyone present seemed caught up in it. There was a palpable sense of pride, but more remarkable was a realisation that the people there, myself included, felt more like participants than guests, as if they were somehow part of the occasion being marked as opposed to mere flag-waving guests at an old woman's party by proxy (I don't believe she was actually there). Consider, also, that the event unfolded at a time when a Conservative-led 'coalition' Government had recently embarked upon an unprecedented demonisation of the poor in this country and somehow, with the help of tax-avoiding billionaire newspaper owners, succeeded in encouraging many British people to blame their equals and inferiors for economic problems caused by rapacious financial institutions and unregulated banks. It was, in other words, a strange moment for forelock-tugging to have suddenly become fashionable again; for undemocratic, unaccountable, unearned and inherited authority, let alone wealth, to be so resolutely unquestioned.

Or was it? In many ways the phrase that resonated through many minds that day should have reminded us that the coin which has hate-filled, xenophobic scaremongering on one side invariably has the sort of patriotism Dr Johnson was referring to on the other. The very notion of 'For Queen and Country' brooks no questioning, no assessment of what is right or what is wrong. It allows no consultation of a moral compass and offers no answer to the question 'why?' The sort of blind, tribal loyalty it encourages and engenders — and has to engender if a nation is, for example, ever to send thousands of young men to die in an incomprehensible war with their own king's cousin — has been making humans feel special, superior, righteous and warlike since pretty much the dawn of time.

The sort of courage that Tennyson refers to in 'The Charge of the Light Brigade' — 'Theirs not to reason why, theirs but to do and die' — is surely as tragic as it is noble, but it could never be mustered if soldiers allowed, say, their humanity to supersede their nationality. For instance, if they were more concerned with the content of an order — its fairness, its intelligence — than they were with the nationality of the crown from which the order ultimately issued. And it is, weirdly, the nationality of the crown at issue here, rather than the nationality of the person wearing it. The only 'British' thing about the royal family that sent hundreds of thousands of British men to fight against Germans in the two world wars was the name they adopted to distract us from the fact that they were as German as the people killing our fathers and sons. A name, of course, they borrowed from their favourite castle.

Do you see how easy it is to be 'unpatriotic'? How obnoxious it could be made to sound in the right hands? What do the above paragraphs display? A denigration of the sacrifices made by men who laid down their lives for 'King and Country'? It would be easy to construct such a conclusion. But what, really, do the words convey? Facts, certainly; a little political opinion, probably; some enduring truths, possibly. What is surely unquestionable is the notion that a population could never be persuaded to die for a cause it barely understands unless it had been successfully convinced that it was somehow special simply by dint of having been born somewhere specific. No matter that the enemy has been equally convinced of an identical belief in the inherent superiority of different birthplaces: they are wrong because they are foreign and we are right because, well, we are not.

Of course, brave West Indian soldiers, Polish fighter pilots, Gurkhas and countless other people who fought for 'us' rather confuse this binary issue, which is why so little attention is paid to them by the sort of 'patriots' who start singing about the Queen with the same breath they use to abuse their West Indian, Polish or Nepalese neighbours. And, of course, by the sort of politicians, patricians and 'patriots' from the other end of the social order who smilingly encourage them.

It seems, then, that any attempt to understand this irrational and ugly fear of an unspecified 'them' demands a better understanding of what it is to be 'us'. We march to war against a foreign power in the name of a monarch whose veins flow with precisely the 'foreign' blood we are being exhorted to shed, and feel no confusion or conflict. Worse, we send white feathers to anyone unpersuaded by the necessity of shedding that blood and christen them 'coward', when to swim against a tide or to fight against the herd invariably involves more gumption and courage than following it.

Less than a hundred years before the First World War, elderly Scottish men who had fought for 'King and Country' in the Napoleonic wars were cleared from their island and Highland homes and effectively deported by landowners motivated only by the knowledge that sheep would prove more profitable inhabitants of the land than humans. The 'deported' were the lucky ones. Many died during bloody evictions. Could a victorious Kaiser really have treated them any worse? Possibly, but why do actual horrors visited upon us by our own rulers always pale in comparison to speculative ones apparently planned by foreign rulers? Easy. Patriotism.

Similarly in England, the Victorian era is still widely seen as a golden age when Britannia ruled the waves. It is the era pub bores most obviously refer to when they talk of days when Britain was still 'Great'. It is probably the greatest mainstay of contemporary 'patriotism'. But that history was not written by the children who worked seven days a week in one of William Blake's 'dark Satanic mills' or by the residents of workhouses or debtors' prisons. Our island history is one of almost unrelenting exploitation of the have-nots by the haves and yet the sheer scale of the offence is diluted in every age by the successful casting of aliens — Jews; Huguenots; Bangladeshis; Irish; Scottish; Pakistanis; West Indians; Poles; Romanians; Muslims — as being somehow more responsible for the have-nots not having than the haves are. Indeed, the only time the exploitation lets up and ordinary men and women are treated with a sort of respect and some gratitude by the ruling classes is when they're being encouraged to lay down their lives 'For Queen and Country'.

It's a bit inflammatory, all that, I grant you, possibly even a little undergraduate in its simplistic idealism, but if it contains even a grain of truth then you have to ask yourself who benefits most from the portrayal of the 'foreigner' as the architect of domestic inequality? Is it the foreigner? Is it the native? Or is it, perhaps, the real architects and beneficiaries of epic inequality and their pocket-filling, fame-hungry friends in politics and the media? I hope that's a rhetorical question but my wonderful, frustrating, exciting, illuminating job on the radio has taught me that, for many, it won't be.

So what does it mean to be British, to be English, to be Scottish, to be Welsh? In 2014, a nasty little story came out about football bosses indulging in racist and misogynistic 'banter' unacceptable even by their profession's dismal standards. A young Welshman of Somali extraction complained that his Scottish manager would often 'joke' about him being Egyptian and claim that young fans of colour gathered at the training ground gates must be his 'brothers'.

With quiet dignity the footballer explained: 'I'm not Egyptian. I'm Welsh. And my parents are from Somalia.' He is Welsh because he wants to be, British because he wants to be and both because he says so.

And that, really, is where this chapter should end. But it won't. What strikes me as a simple statement of a simple fact will strike others as nothing of the sort. As an Englishman of Irish extraction with friends, neighbours and relatives who share my nationality but have parents from Nigeria, Pakistan and Poland, I know that this is the point at which some people, almost certainly ignorant of their own family tree, will point out that if a cow is born in a stable it is not a horse and, inevitably, that the racist bully of a football manager is a victim of 'political correctness gone mad' in a country where 'you're not allowed to say what you think any more'. In that sense, I'm not sure this chapter will ever be over but it's obvious that the people who bleat about 'political correctness' are the ones most terrified of having their opinions properly examined and, encouragingly in a perverse way, most ashamed of what they know will be unearthed. It's obvious, in other words, that their peculiar brand of patriotism is indeed the last refuge of a scoundrel.

5
'You can't talk about immigration ...'

You don't have to be a radio phone-in host to be familiar with the refrain: 'You can't talk about immigration without being called a racist', but it's unlikely anyone else hears it more often. Oddly, it sometimes seems as if the phone-in genre exists on an unleavened diet of immigration conversations — along with 'Is there anybody old out there feeling poorly?' or 'Have you received a parking ticket you don't think you deserved?', no subject is better guaranteed to make the phones ring off the proverbial hook. Yet even while we sometimes seem to speak of little else, folk still insist that they are somehow being prevented from discussing the issue. Recently, moreover, journalists and politicians who should (and almost certainly do) know better have added to these ludicrous claims of some sort of conspiracy of silence while conveniently ignoring the fact that the only people who can't talk about immigration without being called racist are, simply put, the people who can't talk about immigration without being racist.

From a purely professional perspective, I

love racists. The objectors to all immigration and detesters of all foreigners who happily admit to their prejudices (often while claiming that everyone suffers similarly but lacks the courage or clarity to admit it) are, with the possible exception of homophobes who insist on claiming that the Bible supports their stance, my favourite callers of all time. The very mention of 'indigenous tribes of northern Europe' will, for example, have me beaming in anticipation of imminent sport. The more that ring in, the merrier the game and while it's not necessarily an attractive personality trait that lets me take such pleasure in exposing and then ridiculing another's idiocy, it indubitably takes two to tango. There is, after all, no better proof of the daftness of the notion of a 'master race' than the people who claim to belong to it.

But people who in recent years have claimed that their concerns about immigration have been ignored (again, conveniently ignoring the fact that the national conversation rarely seems to be about anything else) are less fun. Often, their level of delusion is quite scary. They want to be free to state, for example, that they consider a neighbour's race to be intrinsic to their desirability as neighbours but they deeply — and, I think, sincerely — resent being called racist for doing so. They want to employ the language and tactics of 1950's bigotry — whether jokes about 'Slopes' and 'Ting-Tongs' or an avowed affection for golliwog dolls — while being somehow excused from all the baggage that such language and iconography inevitably imports. 'Why can't I have a doll that mocks the smiling, simple, pliant black man?' they seem to ask. It doesn't mean *I'm* mocking racial stereotypes. Why can't I employ the language of the nasty, vicious racists of yesteryear? It doesn't mean *I'm* a racist. Why on earth, I invariably wonder, *would you want to*? And why, when it has been explained that your 'innocent' desires cause offence and hurt to others, *would you want to even more than before*?

Of all the initially impenetrable positions one encounters when taking a few hundred calls a month from people who come from every conceivable background, this, to me, has proved the hardest to understand and, in so many ways, the saddest. Neither am I exaggerating. You might not see much logic behind the claim that a debate about immigration has somehow been stifled by a moratorium on golliwog dolls and offensive nomenclature, but ask the people who 'can't talk about immigration without being called racist' what they feel prevented from pronouncing upon and these issues, time and time again, are the ones to which they refer. Recently, empowered by a political climate in which soundbites and demagogues flourish, they have gone further. Why can't I say that I don't want to live next door to Romanians or Pakistanis or Poles? It doesn't make me racist.

It is important to stress here that my position is the inevitable upshot of being a member of something called a 'metropolitan elite'. Roughly translated, this means that I live in a city and have enjoyed a high level of education. By dint of the former I have spent all of my adult life in one of the most emigrated-to cities on the planet, and by dint of the latter I have spent much of that time cogitating and contemplating the gulf between observable fact and incitable feeling. Put the two together, though, and a member of the 'metropolitan elite' comes to mean someone who cannot possibly understand the negative impacts of immigration *because he lives bang in the middle of it* and yet simultaneously *can't see the truth because he sets too much store by facts and figures.* That sounds unkind. It probably is. I'm especially uncomfortable with the idea it throws up that a lack of education is somehow the responsibility of the sufferer. But the notion that educated people who live in cities full of immigrants are less qualified to comment on the issue than less-educated people who live in areas where there aren't any is a nut too tough to be cracked by kindness.

It's important also to note here that metropolitan non-elites (for want of a better phrase) routinely suffer from the same immigration blindness as their well-educated urban counterparts, while non-metropolitan elites (for want... etc.) tend to be less scared of foreigners than their fellow, less-educated country-dwellers. It's not exactly rocket science. The more enlightened you are by education and/or the more exposed you are to the actual reality of living and working alongside people from every corner of the globe, the less seriously you will take the person telling you that they want to squat your spare room or steal your sausages. But you can't say any of this these days without being called 'metropolitan elite'. It's political correctness gone mad, I tell you. Or something like that.

So the people most likely to complain about not being able to talk about immigration without being called racist are really pleading for a new definition of racism. Indeed, they will often 'innocently' ask what racism *really* means. They want to be able to make generalisations and judgments based on ethnicity or colour or country of origin but they want to do so without being called 'racist'. And they want to talk about immigration, employing that same prejudiced vocabulary, without being called 'racist' too. Which is easy to do if you confine yourself to observable facts and leaven unpleasant experiences with pleasant ones; if you avoid generalisations and exaggerations; if, in other words, you approach the issue with an open mind.

Approach it with a closed mind — using fraudulent newspaper headlines as gospel truth; using daft anecdotes as evidential proof; using the presence of any immigrant as proof that there are 'too many' or the crimes of one as proof of the criminality of them all — and you will indeed find it almost impossible to talk about immigration without being called racist. There's a very good reason for that. The word describes a mindset. People who can't talk about immigration without being called racist happily employ the mindset, even boast about doing so, but object furiously to the word used to describe it. I don't know why. Presumably being called racist hasn't always felt as insulting as it does today? I told you it was impenetrable.

So how to help? Because another symptom of the 'metropolitan elite' syndrome is the belief that most people don't really want to be weighed down by these fears and furies. This is usually referred to as possessing a 'bleeding heart' or being a 'liberal do-gooder' and while it's possible that the world would be a better place if it contained even more hatred, bigotry and violence, 'metropolitan elites' look through their own windows on their own communities and tend to believe otherwise.

The best question I've formulated to address this issue is pretty simple: 'How has immigration affected you personally?' It is the privilege of the rambunctious phone-in host to insist that respondents don't stray from the 'personally' element of the question. Thus arresting headlines about a nationwide shortage of school places only apply if you or your child or grandchild etc. has actually failed to secure a place at any school. Talk of the health service being similarly squeezed by 'immigration' is only allowed if you have never encountered an immigrant at the other end of the stethoscope or syringe. If your job really has been taken or your wages lowered by someone who came here with no contacts or employment history and a poor grasp of the language, then the blame surely lies more with you than him. Crime 'sprees' are only relevant if no other nationality commits the same crimes or if you truly feel more aggrieved at being robbed by a Bulgarian than you do by a Brummie. And if you really do feel that way, if you really think the moral value or material impact of any act is in any way affected by the ethnicity of the person doing it, if you'd rather get mugged or treated for cancer by a Brit than a foreigner then you are, under just about any definition around, going to get called a racist. And not just by the 'metropolitan elite'.

6
If the cap fits

Time, perhaps, for an overdue and probably doomed attempt to alleviate some of the 'holier than thou' preaching that may have polluted previous pages. Time, in other words, to examine my own apparently racial prejudices and objections to some forms of immigration. How, drawing exclusively upon genuine personal experience or observable statistical fact, can I justify the ugly feelings prompted within me by the regular appearance of an impromptu and invariably filthy campsite on a traffic reservation near London's Hyde Park? It is populated, we are told and have no real reason to doubt, by 'Roma' or Romani families keen to enjoy the rich seasonal pickings afforded by Britain's capital to pickpockets, beggars and worse.

It's important to do this because, what with possessing a bleeding heart and being an incurable do-gooder and all, I can't help but think that most people who fall into the carefully laid traps of racial stereotyping and immigration scaremongering are perfectly nice, often warm and invariably friendly. I'm conscious that this may sound patronising but, as we've seen, there is surely a big difference between someone who tells a lie in pursuit of fame and fortune, however paltry and transitory, and someone guilty of simply believing it. It's the difference, if you like, between people who really, really want it to be true that foreigners are taking over and riding roughshod over our country and 'values', as opposed to people who think they are but would love to be persuaded that they are not, who would rather see their own niceness, warmth and friendliness reflected back at them from the outside world. Ten minutes of listening to my show or reading my Twitter feed on the right day will show you the difference.

Now I believe, for example, that the humans living temporarily in the conditions described above are indeed Roma and, moreover, that this means they really are possessed of a world view that is utterly alien to me. An Irish traveller explained to me once that the surprising significance of the hedgehog in their folklore (not to mention cuisine) is borne of the belief that they too exist in the hedgerows of society, outside the parameters within which the rest of us live. I haven't encountered the equivalent explanation in Roma culture but it must be pretty similar, validating as it does a rejection of the received social order and the concepts of ownership and criminality this necessarily entails.

This is galling in the extreme. I pay my taxes, obey most laws and endeavour as much as I can to do right by my fellow man, partly, at least, because that is the best way to benefit from the protections that belonging to a society confers upon me. To see someone, anyone, apparently enjoying those protections and privileges while simultaneously rejoicing in their refusal to play by the rules — a refusal to sign their half of the social contract, if you like — truly sticks in the craw. It doesn't really matter how big the problem is — how many people behave in this way — the fact that someone, anyone, does is enough to start a bonfire of resentment in our breasts. Its flames, by the way, look strikingly similar to those burning around successful attempts to typify all unemployed people as, to coin a phrase, 'feckless, workshy layabouts with flat-screen TVs and expensive trainers'. We will, however, usually see those flames extinguished when we — or someone we know — become unemployed. Them or us suddenly becoming Roma is, to say the least, a little less likely.

So I really don't like these people and I think that my dislike is built upon something inextricably allied to their ethnicity or origin or 'culture'. And it's categorically not the same as believing, as we once did, that Jews eat the children of Gentiles or that Protestants deserve to be burned one decade, Catholics the next. No. I have visible, incontrovertible proof that these people really do live in disgusting circumstances and blight my beloved home city. To be honest it's a bit of a leap, for me, to then conclude that this means our national immigration policy must be in tatters. Even the most rabid of the right-wing media can only ever find forty or fifty people who fit the bill and even then only for a few weeks at a time. Indeed, one of the sickest things I've witnessed in the immigration debate was a British politician being taken to Eastern Europe by a TV crew to see the abject squalor in which thousands of Roma families live before concluding that the fact that some of them could feasibly enjoy a vastly superior quality of life in Britain was all the reason needed to ensure that none of them should ever be allowed to come here. The more horrible a foreign child's life, in other words, the less welcome she should be on our shores. The 'politician' was, of course, paid handsomely for the trip.

But I digress. Just because it's a little hard for me to see how a few textbook cases of 'bad immigrants' could spawn certainty about the undesirability of lots more, doesn't mean it's impossible. And with Roma it often seems that all the usual brakes upon prejudice and stereotyping are disengaged. This is partly because the behaviours can be so abhorrent and partly, I think, because the prospect of full assimilation or integration is so slight. Aspects of Islamophobia and anti-semitism (which, as we will see, has a horrible but little-realised historical connection with the persecution of Roma) can be similarly understood: to set yourself apart, to celebrate your otherness, to seek to live by your own rules is to invite the suspicion and opprobrium of the mainstream.

But society's rules transcend these rules. The British judicial system supersedes Beth Din or Sharia courts and, whatever the usual suspects may suggest for the usual self-aggrandising reasons, it will always do so. What we need when confronted with behaviours (or even people) who offend our sensibilities and break our laws is to remind ourselves what we believe in, not obsess about what they do not. It is illegal to pick pockets, it is illegal to beg, if someone does so with a child they risk losing that child, if that child is found to have been 'drugged' (Google it) then that risk is greatly increased. We have a rich and fertile constitution in this country, strengthened by dint of being unwritten and rescued from anachronism, abuse or redundancy by, amongst many modernising factors, our subscription to Winston Churchill's understandably beloved European convention on human rights. Roma may seek to live by rules different from those followed by you and me. It doesn't mean they can. Last time my bus took me past that obnoxious traffic island near London's Hyde Park, it was empty. And yet the resentment and anger, if I'm honest, remained.

Until, only last week, I found myself reading a first-rate thriller which introduced me to the word *Porajmos*. It is a Roma word, best translated as 'the devouring', and it is the word Roma people use to describe what was done to them by the Nazis. Just as Jews were targeted, as were homosexuals and the disabled, Roma were sentenced to death because they were perceived as seeking to exist somehow outside the homogenous mainstream. Because their traditions and customs and behaviours were judged at best impenetrable, at worst abhorrent, they were murdered in their thousands. Because they were so determinedly and obviously different, so alien, so fundamentally other, they were herded onto trains and into gas chambers. A huge proportion of the Roma population was murdered by the Nazis during the Second World War and, while I hesitate to tar you with the same brush of ignorance, I with a bunch of A-Levels and a decent degree and a supposed love of learning did not have a bloody clue until I read about it in a thriller last week.

So next time they are held up as an example of a somehow acceptable racism; as people whose often outrageous behaviour somehow permits us to be vile in a way we would not be about anyone else; next time crime figures are massaged to lay even more blame than they deserve at their feet, ask yourself precisely how big a blight these sorry people really are upon your life, how keen you would be to swap places with them. If you've just had your pocket picked or your cashpoint card cloned or your trip up West spoiled by the sight of a begging child, ask yourself again. And if you've just driven past that roundabout near Hyde Park and seen that they're back with their dirty habits and their criminal intentions and their feral children and the tabloids and the demagogues and the six-figure salaried politicians are encouraging you to hate, ask yourself how you think the *Porajmos* might have started and then ask yourself whether you would have joined in. It works for me.

7
Infidel-ity

My eight-year-old has a sign on her bedroom door that states: 'No Adults Allowed'. It carries precisely the same legal and intellectual weight as a homemade sticker on an East London lamp-post claiming 'Sharia Law Applies in this Area' or a poster in an Orthodox Jewish enclave a couple of miles away insisting that 'Women Must Walk on this Side of the Street'. So why are the reactions to these three signs so spectacularly different?

The answer, I hope obviously, is that we are currently conditioned to be a lot more fearful of Muslims, for whom Sharia is a form of religious law with widely debated dictates, than we are of Orthodox Jews or eight-year-old girls. So it is that when wave after wave of child sex abuse scandals crashed across our country in recent years, it was a very specific type that drew the strongest condemnations and most frenzied outrage. When someone from a foreign or non-Christian background does something bad it is somehow worse than when anyone else does *exactly the same thing.*

This poses two very serious problems: first,

people keen to combat prejudice but lacking, for want of a better description, the intellectual confidence to properly recognise it will deliberately treat ethnic offenders more leniently than others to counterbalance the situation. The phrase 'political correctness' for once comes close to being meaningful here, and there are documented cases of investigations being inadequately pursued precisely because some professionals were fearful of racism accusations. If, in other words, some people pursue the notion that abusers abuse somehow *because* of their ethnicity, others will push back with a well-meaning but equally dangerous response. Treat them more stringently than anyone else because they're from a different ethnic background on the one side, treat them less stringently than anyone else because of their ethnicity on the other. And because ethnicity or religion can clearly have no bearing on sexual 'preferences' unless you are determined to believe differently to shore up pre-existing prejudices, everybody free from such prejudices is in danger of unwittingly disbelieving or dismissing allegations involving the demonised minority that may actually be true.

The same sorry cases also detail victims being treated with contempt and incompetence by police and social workers, but this is less examined because it is less inflammatory, especially in newspapers where the sexualisation of young girls is commercially successful.

Some very prominent columnists and commentators, meanwhile, continue to sneer at the makers of 'historical' child sex abuse allegations, claiming that a victim must be seeking compensation or that being raped as a young teenager can't have been that traumatic if it's taken her twenty years to come forward. They are, in other words, disbelieving and dismissive of a victim's claims but reach sanctimoniously for the 'political correctness' blindfold when other agencies or individuals are guilty of *exactly the same thing*. The only difference being that the abusers of the victims they condemn were pop stars and TV presenters, the abusers of the victims they champion just immigrants. Worse, perhaps, when a teacher absconds with his teenage 'lover', my phone-lines will light up with people keen to defend him, to recount similar experiences, to talk of star-crossed lovers. That teacher, of course, has committed precisely the same offences as the leader of a 'grooming gang' but you wouldn't know it to look at the coverage or the public reaction.

Second, the offence itself becomes very deliberately associated with being from a particular ethnic background as opposed to being criminal, disgusting and wrong. Catholic priests, scout leaders, private school teachers and even DJs are all over-represented in cases of adults abusing boys and girls too young to consent to any sexual activity, but these groups suffer from little or no generalisation or stigmatisation. Never mind, for now, the fact that a child is much, much more likely to be abused by a family member than anyone else, the promotion of the notion that certain ethnicities are more likely to be child abusers is about as rancid as racist rhetoric can get. And yet many people who would balk at having their opinions described thus have been cajoled into holding them.

I realise, as I write this, that not everyone enjoys my daily contact with self-appointed guardians of 'British' values but I assure you, if my words seem unbelievable or exaggerated or stupid, that a cursory glance at the Internet activity of far-right groups and their supporters will yield more Koranic citations and 'understanding' of Medieval Middle Eastern history than the average university degree course.

Remarkably, if you trace this line of thought back to its most basic premise, you unearth a logical deduction that would presumably terrify everyone who spouts the nonsensical notion of a faith or ethnicity somehow increasing the likelihood of paedophilic tendencies. I can state with absolute certainty that no book on the planet, whether religious, technical or a graphic blooming novel, could make me sexually attracted to a child. Similarly, the 'example' of no human being could render me a paedophile. If it emerged that one of my heroes, whether J. D. Salinger or George Orwell or Bill Hicks, had abused children, the idea that it could somehow encourage me to do the same is palpably absurd. So when a member of the far right contends that a religious text could somehow render its adherents paedophiles, they are acknowledging the possibility that a book or a human role model is capable of creating a sexual attraction to children in the reader or admirer that would not otherwise have existed. I hope you can dismiss this possibility with absolute confidence because we only have to apply the idea to ourselves to realise that this is not true. One cannot help wondering what lurks in the minds of people apparently convinced that sexual attraction to children can be somehow 'switched on' by a book or another person's behaviour. As most hardcore homophobes seem ultimately more terrified by their own secret desires than anything else, so people promulgating the idea that paedophilia is a lifestyle choice may be saying more about themselves than anyone else.

None of which explains why a particular type of child sex abuser, members of the so-called 'grooming gangs', do routinely share similar backgrounds. The answer, I think, is breathtakingly simple, although I doubt I could have arrived at it without the luxury of being able to invite callers onto my programme from that shared background.

The first thing to understand is that the largely Pakistani grooming gangs whose crimes have been accurately if rather disproportionately reported in recent years are not paedophiles from their point of view. The age of consent varies between countries.

The second part of the problem is that generally in the West, we know that if we were found guilty of a crime such as underage sex, even in a society that in many ways normalises the notion of underage girls being sexually desirable (remember the countdown to the singer becoming legal?), we would not tell anyone. We would be ashamed.

It seems to me inarguable that some men

from a particular background, where traditions and practices have been imported from parts of rural Pakistan, feel no such shame. The behaviour is normalised to such a degree that they can invite their cousins and colleagues to join the abuse with no fear of being condemned and reported. This speaks of an attitude toward women that is as widespread within these communities as it is contemptible. It is the backdrop to forced marriage, to so-called honour killing and to female genital mutilation. It is also a backdrop that lies behind just about every society in history if you take the time to look back far enough. Daughters and wives who effectively 'belong' to their fathers and husbands can be found everywhere from the Bible to the pages of Jane Austen. A political party operating in Britain today accepts large donations from a man who believes that a man cannot rape a woman to whom he is married, that she cannot refuse him. 'Christian' marriage regularly sees the wife promise to 'honour and obey' her husband but not the other way round. Irish girls were locked up in grisly institutions for decades for the crime of having had sex and got pregnant in 'communities' where a priest's word was law and where, we now know, many of those same priests were sexually abusing children on an epic scale.

It is not a religion or an ethnicity that empowered 'grooming gangs' to commit their crimes, then, it is misogyny pure and simple. And while all religions struggle to accommodate modern notions of gender equality, it has no more to do with any one religion these days than denying all British women the vote until 1928 had to do with Christianity. Nobody should forget or overlook the plain fact that in one case the judge told the abusers that one of the factors in the abuse was that 'the victims were not part of your community or religion.' But to focus exclusively on this aspect of the grooming process is to distract from other equally grim factors and deliberately duck the fact that their modus operandi and motivation do not differ substantively from those of all groomers, whatever their background. Thus in a predominantly white society most, but by no means all, of their victims will be white, and the blue touch paper of racist rhetoric is once again ignited. If we don't blow it out, though, we add insult to the victims' injuries by using their plight to score ugly political points.

We also, unwittingly, let the offenders off the hook while punishing the innocent. These men did these things because they are misogynistic, vicious and terrified by strong, independent females. Suggest that they did it *because* they are from a different cultural background and you not only give life to the lie that they somehow couldn't help themselves, you also implicitly condemn as complicit all the people from that same background who are just as repulsed and disgusted by these crimes as you are. And that is almost all of them. And that, once again, is exactly what the disseminators of 'Loathe Thy Neighbour' politics want. Gerard Batten has even called for every Muslim in the country to sign a 'code of conduct'. He, incidentally, still sits in the European Parliament on benches from which former colleague Godfrey Bloom was expelled by the party leadership for calling women 'sluts'. And yes, that would be the self-same party that accepted money from Demetri Marchessini, the man who believes it impossible for a husband to rape his wife. You couldn't, as they say, make it up.

8
Taking the biscuit

A billionaire, a politician, an Englishman and an immigrant are seated at a table. On the table is a plate and on the plate are ten biscuits. The billionaire trousers nine of them and slips a couple to the politician, who leans towards the Englishman and whispers in his ear: 'Look out! That immigrant is trying to nick your biscuit.'

This, it seems to me, is a pretty neat encapsulation of the political discourse in this country at the moment. And, my gosh, that billionaire/politician alliance is working rather well. Voters polled across the generational and financial divides routinely report that immigration is among their chief concerns and yet when you ask them why — as I have had the privilege of doing for more than ten years on a radio phone-in show with the busiest switchboard in the business — they very rarely offer up any evidence more powerful than the phantom biscuit-nicker.

This leaves other politicians and pundits with a difficult choice: enter into a competition to see who can promise to come down hardest on the phantom biscuit-nicker; ignore the issue because the biscuit-nicker is, well, a phantom; or try to explain to people how they are being deliberately and cynically manipulated into blaming entirely the wrong people for their problems.

Option one, a race to the bottom, is currently the most popular. It is an unwinnable race but politicians of just about every hue have decided to address what voters think rather than what voters know. You can hardly blame them. It is not easy to tell angry, frightened people persuaded that their lonely biscuit is under threat from a foreigner that they should be more concerned about the whereabouts of nine that have already disappeared. Add to the mix the journalists and commentators who are also enjoying a few choice crumbs from the billionaire's table and you have an environment in which option two, ignoring the issue because it is not really an issue, becomes impossible. Meanwhile, suggesting that we should look at rich people to understand why we are poor — rather than people even poorer than us — is downright dangerous.

So option three, to tell the truth and shame the devil, involves telling voters that they are wrong and gullible. It is, moreover, almost impossible to deliver that message in the context of immigration without also seeming to add 'xenophobic' to the list of accusations. We don't really need to wonder why most politicians fight a little shy of this! It's why the ones who aren't actually motivated by ugly prejudice, but see the success of those who are, end up sounding so half-hearted when promising to 'clamp down' on the problem. They know there isn't a problem on anything like the scale the voters believe but also that as long as the voters cling to their beliefs they ignore or dismiss them at their peril.

And so politics becomes pointless in almost any meaningful or constructive sense. When the immigration myth is allowed to take hold on such a grand scale, politician and voter can blame it for literally everything. Health Service struggling? Blame immigration. Bolshy, workshy daughter can't get a job? Blame an immigrant who can. House too small or expensive? Blame immigration. Wages too low? Blame immigration. I could go on, but you get the picture: immigration can, in the right hands, be blamed for just about everything that anyone is unhappy or uncomfortable about. And a politician with the right blend of bonhomie and plausibility can grow rich and famous by doing precisely that. The voters even get gulled into thinking he or she is on their 'side', with immigrants somehow on the other. Who really benefits from this fraudulent apportioning of responsibility for social or economic problems? Easy.

Eighty-five identified individuals currently enjoy the same amount of the world's total wealth, approximately £1 trillion, as the poorest three and a half billion. Just think about that. Half of the world's population can lay claim to the same sum as just eighty-five billionaires. They are not all media moguls and plutocrats hell-bent on driving us all back to the days of feudalism and land clearances but they are generally driven by a belief that no amount of money is ever 'enough'. I imagine it would be almost impossible to amass a fortune of that size if you weren't driven by a burning desire for more, more, more. Modern capitalism is predicated on infinite growth — it's why a company reporting a dip in profits from, say, £300 million to £250 million is 'bad' news — but resources are resolutely finite. If the billionaire wants to get even richer, the money has to come from somewhere and the chances are it will come from you.

Could anything suit his project better than a political climate in which 'foreigners' or 'immigrants' or 'migrants' are routinely blamed for our problems? I can't think of anything. And as long as they are blamed what prospect is there of any of the problems they stand accused of causing actually being fixed? None. But the billionaires and their lapdogs in the media and politics don't care. They just need to keep up the illusion that they have *our* best interests at heart by continuing to heap scorn on people defined by *their* otherness, by their origins, by their arbitrary differences.

Look at the language. Five hundred 'migrants' recently died on a ship sunk by people smugglers after their human cargo dared to complain. Actually, of course, five hundred mothers, fathers, sons and daughters died. Five hundred possessors of dreams and emotions and personalities every bit as rounded and contrary as yours and mine. Five hundred people, in other words, who are exactly like us but who happened to be born in a part of the world so awful that they were prepared to risk *absolutely everything* in the hope of getting to somewhere safe and relatively prosperous. Some of the people who already live there, however, have been convinced that their safety and prosperity is under mortal threat from these people who want nothing more than to share in and cherish it, who are likely to value it a lot more than those of us who take it for granted because it is all we have ever known.

We hear daily *from the same people* how we

must stop 'bashing bankers'; how seeking a society in which a boss earns, say, twenty-five times what her worst-paid employee does instead of two hundred times is the 'politics of envy'; how food banks and payday loan companies and bailiffs only exist because of our fellow citizens' fecklessness and irresponsibility. We never think they are talking about us when we swallow this rhetoric until our lives hit the buffers and we realise that they were talking about us all along. They know that the best way to distract our attention from their own responsibility for injustice and inequality and increasingly medieval distributions of wealth is to identify and castigate a scapegoat. And they know that there is no more effective scapegoat than the faceless, voiceless, blameless immigrant: the neighbour they want us to loathe.

How has it come to this? How, after seeing the history of hatred repeat itself again and again across the centuries, have we not learned to see more clearly? The answer is, was and for ever will be the same: it always suits someone to have the rest of us blaming each other for our problems and punching down in the hope of solving them. There will always be someone happy to reap the rewards of division and enmity, whatever the real costs to the rest of us. And there will always be people who love injustice, who love inequality and who love a status quo that sees more and more of the planet's wealth moving to fewer and fewer people. We will never land a punch on them while we are being so cynically and successfully persuaded that they're on our side and that the real villains of the piece are those immigrants over there with their beady little eyes on our biscuits. Ask who is doing the persuading, ask what is in it for them, ask who is paying their wages and then ask yourself this: whose side do you think they are really on?

About LBC

LBC is Britain's only national news talk radio station. It tackles the big issues of the day, with intelligent, informed and provocative opinion from guests, listeners and presenters, including Nick Ferrari, James O'Brien, Shelagh Fogarty, Iain Dale, Ken Livingstone, David Mellor and Beverley Turner. LBC reaches 1.2 million people in Britain and is available on DAB digital radio, online at lbc.co.uk, through mobile apps, Sky Digital Channel 0112, Virgin Media Channel 919 and on 97.3FM in London.

About the Series

In this major new series, popular LBC presenters tackle the big issues in politics, current affairs and society. We might applaud their views; we might be outraged. But these short, sharp polemics are destined to generate controversy, discussion and debate — and lead Britain's conversation.

Titles in the series
Steve Allen, *So You Want to Be a Celebrity?*
Duncan Barkes, *The Dumbing Down of Britain*
Iain Dale, *The NHS: Things That Need to Be Said*
Nick Ferrari, *It's Politics ... But Not As We Know It*
James O'Brien, *Loathe Thy Neighbour*

About the Series